Made in the USA
Coppell, TX
09 February 2020

15632387R00049